Our Thoughts Chilled

Savor the Abstract

Jeff Allen Nickles

BookLeaf Publishing

India | USA | UK

Made with ❤ on the BookLeaf Publishing Platform
www.bookleafpub.in
www.bookleafpub.com

Dedication

To Maggie and James,
From before you were born and forever after, you will always be the greatest blessing of my life. I am so proud of the kind and talented young adults you have become. This collection is dedicated to you, with all my love.

-Dad

Preface

I began writing at the age of 14 as a form of therapy and a means to understand my thoughts, emotions, and surroundings. Initially, it helped me navigate those formative years. Later, it evolved into an opportunity to write lyrics in college, which often earned me free drinks. As I grew older, my writings became a way to capture the feelings associated with significant life events, such as the passing of my grandparents, Beatrice and James, and my mother, Pamela. If you're reading this, you're getting an intimate glimpse into my psychology and perspectives—apologies in advance =). I hope it serves to inspire and I hope this finds you well! Tomorrow is vital. At midnight clean, perfect it arrives and hopes we've learned something yesterday. With love/Jeff.

Acknowledgements

Inspired by the support of my loving wife, Charisce
Nickles,

Our children,
Vivian Anderson
Maggie Nickles
James Nickles
Fiona Anderson

.... and my Mom, Pamela Nickles, who chose to give me
life when she was only 15 years old, thank you eternally.

1. Box of Yesterday

Slideshows & dark silhouettes,
Old cowards filled with used days,
Home movies and mix cassettes,
Ten thousand morning sun rays,
Ticket stub memories,
Faded photos stained yesterday,
Hope in all our eyes,
Quiet smile, lost dismay,
Spread across this blanket,
Recollections & blurred truth,
Plans written on learner's permit,
The narrative of our youth.

2. Savor the Abstract

A few steps to the side,
It all goes rushing by,
And closed eyes don't hide,
A head heavy, heart high,
Brace for the impact,
It's the ride more than destination,
So savor the abstract,
Without answer no question,
A rough ride home,
The only one measured,
Several nameless to roam,
To survive the rumored,
Brace for the impact,
It's the ride more than destination,
So savor the abstract,
Without answer no question,
Oppose the written rule,
Fold it like a picture in a wallet,
Memoirs of a chosen fool,
By addiction more than habit,

Brace for the impact,
It's the ride more than destination,
So savor the abstract,
Without answer no question.

3. Manumit

Lay down rest,
Pray pass test,
Gaze ceiling night gone,
Dream awake soon dawn,
Rise work home,
Door road roam
Day week life,
Hope courage knife,
Cause effect apathy,
Feel touch happy,
Root tree seed,
Pen paper bleed,
Try want believe,
Smile cry conceive,
Earn save spend,
Love die defend.

4. Our Thoughts Chilled

In the midst of changing season,
Sit
tight without feeling,
Lost
motive and denied reason,
A
stubborn fool and his believing,
A
diary empty with tomorrows,
A
casualty of last chances,
Satisfying
nightmarish sorrows,
Arsonist
to ones own romances,
Leaves
of life falling,
Changing
colors of personality,
Past

forever left calling,
Remnants
of ancient ability,
A
cork from a fresh bottle,
Pours
our thoughts chilled,
Hopes
like a newborn to coddle,
Aspirations
to be fulfilled,
Another
frame to reference,
Nuzzled
lost in psyche,
Relentless
exertion's recompense,
Blindness,
unless chosen to see.

5. ...a bout with Death

I have looked in your eyes,
Death you don't scare me,
Tears roll from blue eyes,
You have taken from me,

You came silent and raged away,
Faith in need of faith today,
You have stolen, no one can repay,
I have loved, will love beyond today,

Death you don't scare me,
I close my eyes and feel,
I will let you think you beat me,
I close my eyes and heal,

From end beginning always,
That is just earth's gift,
Abrupt, demanding castaways,
Emotions within left to shift,

Driving too fast for conditions,
Road winding up ahead,
Lost in our own superstitions,
Head heavy looking for bed,

Dependable, enduring memory,
Singular action, pay gratitude,
Our lives now led so sincerely,
Every effort, love to exude,

Death you don't scare me,
Only need close my eyes to see,
Their strength, my tranquility,
Forever, always a part of me.

6. Inherent

Eyes sewn wholly shut,
Still, staring at the sun,
The meaning sure cut,
The walking before the run,
The words that were left,
Days with no use,
Ears closed, unnoticed theft,
Revelations with wet fuse,
Intentions forgotten, discarded,
Days wasted, consumed,
Insecurity, so guarded,
Healthier than assumed,
Happier, than before,
Eyes open, now so broad,
Content, central, core,
Firm, but anger thawed.

7. Urbanity

Crimes, personal preservation,
Homes lacking doors,
Infliction devoid of intervention,
Souls twist into whores,
Shots ring out nightly,
Rain washes the blood away,
Streets so cheated, left crying,
A life barely begun, died today.
Soft expression to another mother,
Anger, rage and never a reason,
Witness too rigid to bother
for trepidation of social treason.
It's the same old depressing tale,
The one our cities tell habitually,
Populace absent of escape to avail,
Praying please *no one I know* today.

8. Love, Hope and Sanity

Walk home from the corner bar,
Memories, friends carry us home,
We know, lucky to be this far,
Footsteps in rhythm, adulthood syndrome,
Eyes open, eyes closed,
While traffic rushes close by,
Sidewalk safety, so composed,
Nostalgia held close, to rely,
Cold wind burns our cheek,
As winter slowly kidnaps summer,
Childhood recollections antique,
No cure for our mental cancer,
Careful to care just enough,
As we lunge for trust,
Life is full of contrast, rough,
Intent, always so earnest,
Drink away the cold season,
To numb the pain,
Sober up for warm reason,
Savor the mundane,

Stand tall against it all,
Propped, friends and family,
Guarding against a fall,
All for love, hope and sanity.

9. Son's Lament

Words protected, leftovers not said,
Regret, verses spoken with anger,
Lives altered, weary eyes, tears bled,
Hearts smashed, faulty danger,
Hope inquiries for an afterlife,
Love's laughs fracture to scream,
Censored harm like a concealed knife,
Rapids escaped, passing upstream,
Denial, puzzles with missing pieces,
Moments absent in what remained,
Words, yours in my head, increases,
Pictures, to the past you are chained,
Guarded recollections, like jewelry gold,
Comprehending what you aspired,
Lucky lives led, fortunate stories told,
Amplified, two hearts melded, rewired.

10. Interlude

Strings pulled tight, ring out,
Necks bowed just to hear,
What is this really all about?
Consideration so close, near,
Fingers fast in explanation,
Hearts poured out complete,
Tones settling in desperation,
Notes, this is silence in defeat,
Harmony deliberately steals the moment,
Where fear had crops yet to be farmed,
Our brain, doubt so wasted, time spent,
Melody, a hostage perfectly unharmed,
A symphony of vivid tomorrows,
Chorus piercing thoughts we once knew,
A retirement of wretched sorrows,
Restoration in song, like baby born new.

11. Coconut and Rum

Radio on, shower and out the door,
Summer, small town, a paved
Habit next door,
Down past the last house, two
Days past yesterday, stop
Ask anyone, they will show you
The way, there is a keg again,
No work today, guitars and keg
Stands, nickname replace name,
Old cover bands, 18 year old fame,
The cold season, made this sun welcome,
One more reason, we'll mix
Coconut with rum.
Drowning in sun's rays, midnight
Taco dreams, backroads lit by
Headlight beams, it was a cold
Season, made this son welcome,
One more reason, we'll mix
Coconut with rum.

12. Walk with the Stars

Out into the night to find peace
Walk into the stars, problems cease
Pebble thrown into the sun,
Talk with the man on the moon,
Who we never saw again,
His wisdom calmed the soul, like
a cool breeze tames the heat,
But we envisioned more, answers
to make us complete.
Undaunted we trudged on with reason
to accompany our rhyme,
We visited Orion to get caught in a
moment just on time,
His might intrigued us and we felt
grateful in his presence,
But even with such power his weakness
was created by his essence,
No answer to be found without
question to ask,
Always, forever hope hidden, a

face behind mask.

13. Confide

Two miles traveled, 800 miles to go
An old life left behind, destination unknown,
Hiding in the sunset, find hope in distant skies,
Tomorrow brings another chance, to escape from all
their lies,
I need a new beginning,
To the end of this life I have been living, giving,
To the many whose hands were in mine, by my side,
From yourself no one can every hide, I find,
In me they do confide.
Mountains in front of me, a low place in my rear
view,
Seen enough for death to scare me, nothing left to
prove,
100 miles to Colorado, closer than far away,
Heard enough from my demons, nothing left to say,
I need a new beginning,
To the end of this life I have been living, giving,
To the many whose hands were in mine, I find,
In me they do confide.

14. The Trip and the Fall

Everything a strange numbness, my head,
Struggles with reality, but maybe,
A hallucination instead,
Wasn't prepared, was not ready
when the trip began,
As it continues, I dread it to
end.
Maybe I've been falling my whole
life,
From nowhere, perception piercing
like knife,
Problems have long gone away,
Calendars confused into a new day,
Transform with wings and fly,
You fell today but you did not die.

15. Cannot Change the Past (1993)

Was walking through a forest and came to a large
opening,

The light disappeared into night, in my hands my destiny
I was holding,

My shadow danced in the moonlight, while it told me of
what was to be enstore,

Grabbed my shadow's hand and she led me through a
hidden door,

Inside the light was bright and the mood was mellow, my
shadow gone,

A voice spoke to me leading the way but I wasn't sure
for how long,

Walked toward the voice and it got dimmer, now gone,
suddenly alone,

Gathered motivation from this though, for the rest of my
life have I set the tone?

Reached another door I walked inside and forest again I
was in,

Now as I grow older, I look for that opening, in that
forest, but we'll never see it again.

21

16. Determined (1990)

Driving down the lane,
Crack, my knee, pain,
Pain, severe, cannot see,
Paralyzing me.
Flat on back I lay,
Results await xray,
Emerging smell of fear,
Before it began the end of career,
So heavily sedated,
Events strangely related,
Doctors diagnosis the worst,
I wore it like a curse,
He told me, only time will tell,
My time, passed in recovery hell,
Thought I would die from the heat,
But comeback thoughts played on repeat,
And as I drive the lane once again,
This time I pull up, jumpshot for the win.

17. Fighting for Peace/Contradiction (1991)

A hint of the future, buried in our past,
If you think, you have the key,
Where were you last,
Retrace your steps and you will find me.
We overlooked what we had,
Tricked ourselves, getting by, acting mad,
Now left wondering if the past will resurface,
Awaiting new evidence to enter our case,
Sad, at a time we would have done
anything for each other,
But we committed the worst mistake, we believed
one another.

18. The Future Beckons (1991)

The future is becoming harder to second guess,
It's become cloudy, seeing through opaque glass,
Is there no relief in sight?
Has hope become blacked out by night?
Failure is the only pain of test,
You fail, you heal with deserved rest,
Reach out, if you can spare a hand,
Time just flows as sand,
In life we will twist and we will be turned,
But the real key, always, what have we learned?

19. Real Strength (1991)

Is strength found in height?
measured by might?
powered thru fear,
I am not a believer.
Strength derives from inside,
Courage won't let you hide,
be your own person,
teach others that lesson?
Strength epitomizes heart,
Say what you mean as a start,
Follow the path you know is right,
Example for others taking flight,
Don't succumb to being a follower,
You weren't born to fall over.